What's in this book

This book belongs to

_____

你喜欢什么活动?
What activities do you like?

学习内容 Contents

沟通 Communication

说说活动喜好
Talk about activities that one likes

生词 New words

★	玩	to play
★	活动	activity
★	电视	television
★	踢	to kick
★	足球	football
★	打球	to play ball games
★	还是	or
	玩具	toy
	电脑	computer
	高兴	happy

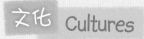

句式 Sentence patterns

你喜欢玩玩具，还是喜欢看电视？
Do you like playing with toys or watching television?

你喜欢吃饼干，还是喜欢做饼干呢？
Do you like eating biscuits or making them?

 Project

调查活动喜好，并完成活动金字塔
Do a survey on activities and finish
the activity pyramid

文化 Cultures

中国传统活动
Traditional Chinese activities

Get ready

1 What do you like to do in your spare time?

2 Do you prefer individual or group activities?

3 What is your favourite activity?

huó dòng
活动

放学回家后，你喜欢做什么活动？

你喜欢玩玩具，还是看电视？

tī
踢

zú qiú
足球

dǎ qiú
打球

你喜欢踢足球吗？喜欢
打球吗？

wán diàn nǎo
玩电脑

很多人喜欢玩电脑，你
觉得怎么样？

gāo xìng

高兴

我喜欢做饼干。和大家
一起分享，我很高兴。

你喜欢吃饼干，还是做
饼干呢？

Let's think

1 Recall the story and match.

2 Circle and say the activities that are in the wrong place.

Outdoor activities

Indoor activities

New words

1 Learn the new words.

活动

打球

足球

踢

玩具

玩

电视

高兴

电脑

还是

2 Write the letters and colour the pictures.

a 打球　　b 看电视　　c 踢足球

听听说说 Listen and say

🎧 03 **1** Listen and circle the correct answers.

🎧 04 **2** Look at the pictures. Listen to the sto

1 男孩喜欢做什么？

   a 打球

   b 看书

   c 玩电脑

2 他们明天做什么？

   a 喝茶

   b 回家

   c 看老虎

3 他们都喜欢什么活动？

   a 看书

   b 打球

   c 玩玩具

① 你回家吗？还是去打球？

我不回家，我和他们去打球。

③ 回家看电视？还是玩电脑？

我回家做饼干。

d say.

Look at the pictures.
Talk about them with
your friend.

她喜欢打球，
还是喜欢玩电脑？

打球！

他喜欢踢足球，
还是喜欢玩玩具？

他喜欢玩玩具。

Task

Talk about after-school activities with your friend.

你喜欢什么活动？

你今天回家做什么？

你和谁一起玩？

我喜欢……

我今天回家……

我和……一起玩。

Game

Shoot the basketballs to see what Hao Hao is writing about his friend. Write the correct letters in the circles.

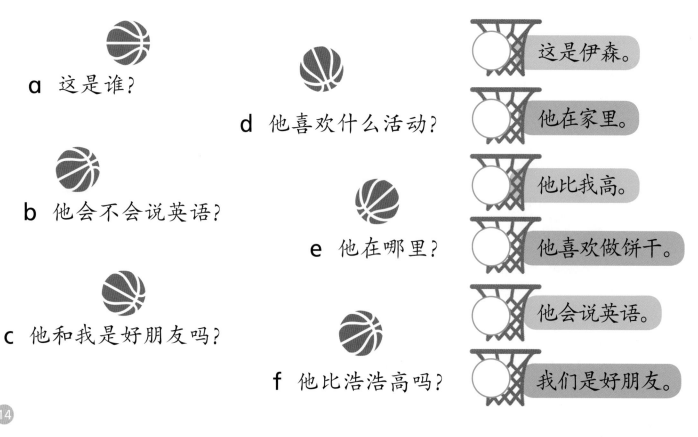

a 这是谁？

b 他会不会说英语？

c 他和我是好朋友吗？

d 他喜欢什么活动？

e 他在哪里？

f 他比浩浩高吗？

这是伊森。

他在家里。

他比我高。

他喜欢做饼干。

他会说英语。

我们是好朋友。

Song

🎧 05 Listen and sing.

我爱看电视，
你喜欢打球，
她爱玩电脑，
他爱踢足球，
喜好不相同，
仍是好朋友。

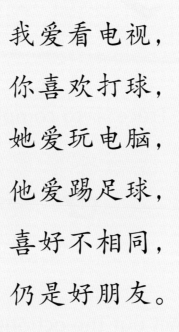

课堂用语 Classroom language

你好

+1

你可以重复吗？
Can you repeat?

15

写一写 Write

1 Review and trace the stroke.

提

2 Learn the component. Trace 扌 to complete the characters.

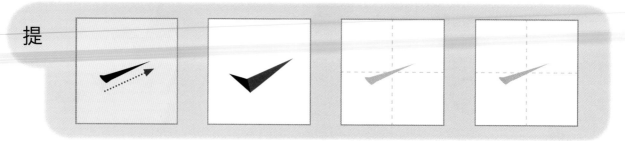

扒　扣　抄　拥

3 Look at the pictures. Act out the actions. Colour 扌 in the characters red.

拥抱

拍打

拉扯

指挥

4 Trace and write the character.

一　丁　扌　打

打 打

一　二　干　王　王　玎　玎　球　球

球 球

球 球

5 Write and say.

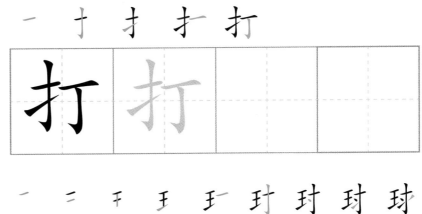

放学后，我们喜欢
一起　　球。

汉字小常识 **Did you know?**

Colour the bottom-left
component red.

Some characters include a
component that is placed on
the left and the bottom part
of a character.

 还  起 翅  迷 这

多元学习 Connections

Cultures

1 Learn about some traditional Chinese activities.

Players hit a lightweight ball back and forth across a table.

Ping-pong

Players play as two armies in a battle to capture the enemy's general.

Chinese chess

T'ai-chi

People practise T'ai-chi, one type of martial arts for defense and health benefits.

Players keep a shuttlecock in the air using their bodies. No hands are allowed!

Jianzi

2 Say the words and ask your friend to do the actions.

打　　　踢　　　看　　　画　　　写

Project

1 Find out what activities your classmates like. Write the numbers.

你喜欢打球，还是喜欢玩电脑？

我喜欢打球，不喜欢玩电脑。

⚽🎾	👤 ⌗⌗ 多少人喜欢？
打球	
唱歌	
玩玩具	
做饼干	
看电视	
玩电脑	
踢足球	

2 How often do you do the activities in a week? Write the numbers in the pyramid. Do you live a healthy life?

你喜欢的活动在上面，还是在下面？

The Activity Pyramid

Cut down on

Twice a week

3-5 times a week

Every-day

 温习 Checkpoint

1 Complete the questions and learn to play with the shuttlecock.

Say 'I am very happy.' in Chinese.

这是什么活动？
Answer in Chinese.

这是什么？
Answer in Chinese.

Say 'How about we play with toys?' in Chinese.

我们去踢足球，还是去玩玩具？

Say 'Do you like singing or painting?' in Chinese.

Complete the word.

球

你喜欢看书，还是看电视？

2 Work with your friend. Colour the stars and the chillies.

Words	说	读	写
玩	☆	☆	🌶
活动	☆	☆	🌶
电视	☆	☆	🌶
踢	☆	☆	🌶
足球	☆	☆	🌶
打球	☆	☆	🌶
还是	☆	☆	🌶
玩具	☆	🌶	🌶
电脑	☆	🌶	🌶
高兴	☆	🌶	🌶

Words and sentences	说	读	写
你喜欢玩玩具，还是喜欢看电视？	☆	🌶	🌶
你喜欢吃饼干，还是喜欢做饼干呢？	☆	🌶	🌶

Talk about activities that one likes	☆

3 What does your teacher say?

My teacher says ...

分享 Sharing

Words I remember

玩	wán	to play
活动	huó dòng	activity
电视	diàn shì	television
踢	tī	to kick
足球	zú qiú	football
打球	dǎ qiú	to play ball games
还是	hái shì	or
玩具	wán jù	toy
电脑	diàn nǎo	computer
高兴	gāo xìng	happy

Other words

放学	fàng xué	school is over
回家	huí jiā	to go home
后	hòu	after, afterwards
很多	hěn duō	many
觉得	jué dé	think of
怎么样	zěn me yàng	how
分享	fēn xiǎng	to share

OXFORD
UNIVERSITY PRESS

Oxford University Press is a department of the University of Oxford.
It furthers the University's objective of excellence in research, scholarship,
and education by publishing worldwide. Oxford is a registered trade mark of
Oxford University Press in the UK and in certain other countries

Published in Hong Kong by
Oxford University Press (China) Limited
39th Floor, One Kowloon, 1 Wang Yuen Street, Kowloon Bay,
Hong Kong

Illustrated by Anne Lee, KK Ng, KY Chan and Wildman

Photographs for reproduction permitted by Dreamstime.com

China National Publications Import & Export (Group) Corporation is an authorized distributor of
Oxford Elementary Chinese.

Please contact content@cnpiec.com.cn or 86-10-65856782

ISBN: 978-0-19-082201-9

10 9 8 7 6 5 4 3 2